Spaghetti & Meatballs: Growing Up Italian

Diana
Pishner
Walker

illustrated by
Ashley Teets

Headline Kids
an imprint of Headline Books, Inc.
Terra Alta, WV

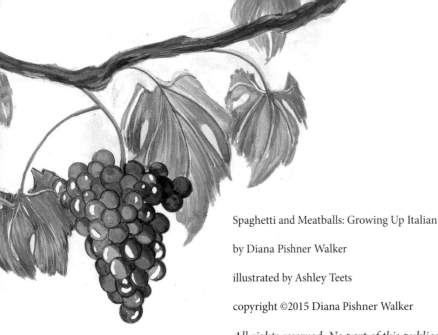

Spaghetti and Meatballs: Growing Up Italian

by Diana Pishner Walker

illustrated by Ashley Teets

copyright ©2015 Diana Pishner Walker

To order additional copies of this book, or for book publishing information, or to contact the author:

Headline Kids
P. O. Box 52
Terra Alta, WV 26764

Tel: 800-570-5951
Email: mybook@headlinebooks.com
www.headlinebooks.com
www.headlinekids.com

Published by Headline Books
Headline Kids is an imprint of Headline Books

ISBN-13: 9781882658367

Library of Congress Control Number: 2015942392

PRINTED IN THE UNITED STATES OF AMERICA

This book is dedicated to my grandparents:
Rosa Spadafora and Giovanni (John) Allessio
San Giovanni in Fiore, Cosenza Italy
and
Maria (Mary) Costa and Dominick Pishner (Piscioneri)
Caulonia (Reggio di Calabria) Italy

My grandparents came from Italy, the country that looks like a boot. They immigrated to the United States in the early 1900s as teenagers and kept the customs and traditions of the 'old country' within their new American family.

ITALY

When I listened to my grandparents' stories about Italy—I found life was different from the way most children grow up today.

Food and family meals were very important. Everyone sat down together at the same time, especially on Sundays.

My parents would take my brother, sister and me to Mass and then to my Allessio, grandparent's house, for lunch. Lunch was always wonderful and included spaghetti and meatballs with freshly baked bread. We talked all afternoon.

My Nonnie, as I called her, loved to crochet. She made hundreds of doilies and always gave me one for my bedroom to take home.

My Papoo always played tricks on us to make us laugh. He had a little box with a picture of a cow on it. When the box was turned over it made a mooing sound. Papoo would turn that little box over behind me and laughed when I jumped. He also liked to put walnuts in our shoes when no one was looking, because we always took off our shoes at the door. Then he would laugh at your surprise when you couldn't put your shoes on. My Papoo didn't speak much English. He and Nonnie spoke to my mom and dad and to each other in Italian. But one thing I can remember him always saying was "POO POO" Pittsburgh and he would laugh. He always wore a little hat and we knew when he took it off it was going to become a pretend camera. He made us laugh and smile every time he acted like he was taking our picture.

My dad's parents, Nonnie and Papoo Pishner, lived close to us. I could go there any time and my Nonnie Pishner was always baking something and often had a pot of pastini on the stove. I thought I could smell all the good things in that kitchen from my house. She made potato pancakes from mashed potatoes. At Christmas, both grandmas and my aunts made fritis, and pita piatas.

My grandparents did not need as much from the store as we did.

They had gardens with tomatoes, peppers, zucchini and green beans. There were grapevines in front of their houses. My cousins and I would just pick grapes right off the vine for snacks. Sometimes we went out to pick berries, too.

I was lucky enough to not only have grandparents but I also had a great-grandpa. He was Grandpa Costa. He lived close to my family, too. Grandpa Costa had a garden and a little farm with chickens and cows. Sometimes those cows got past the fence and Grandpa Costa had to chase them to get them back to his farm. He walked with a cane, so he used the cane to guide them. He loved bananas and read our daily newspaper, mostly to look at the pictures. He spoke no English at all, but we always understood each other.

It was nice to have my grandparents and great grandpa living nearby. I also had an Aunt Mary, Uncle John and cousins—they were our neighbors and Aunt Mary and Uncle John were also my godparents.

The meals and the food were not the only important things to my family. The holidays were very special. When it was Christmas time, my dad took me with him to cut down our Christmas tree. My mother and grandmothers and aunts made all of the fritis, cookies and pita piatas. I remember there was always a bowl of nuts to be cracked and hard, striped candy in bowls at my grandparent's house.

For dinner on Christmas Eve, we ate fish and more fish. We always had at least seven different kinds of fish with our pasta. It took my mom, Nonnie, and my aunts all day to prepare the fish. They each wore their own special apron while they cooked.

After that huge meal, we went to Midnight Mass and it was so hard to stay awake. The church was full and the people were dressed up.

Christmas morning we were all together again for a meal and to open all the gifts. My Aunt Clara, who lived with my Nonnie and Papoo Allessio, worked at a department store that had the most beautiful gift wrapping, making her gifts sometimes too nice to rip open. Uncle John worked at that same store and decorated the store windows. Each year at Christmas time, my mom and dad took us to see his windows.

Easter was another holiday that involved a big celebration in my family and we always had Easter Bread! We went to church on Maundy Thursday, Good Friday and of course, Easter Sunday.

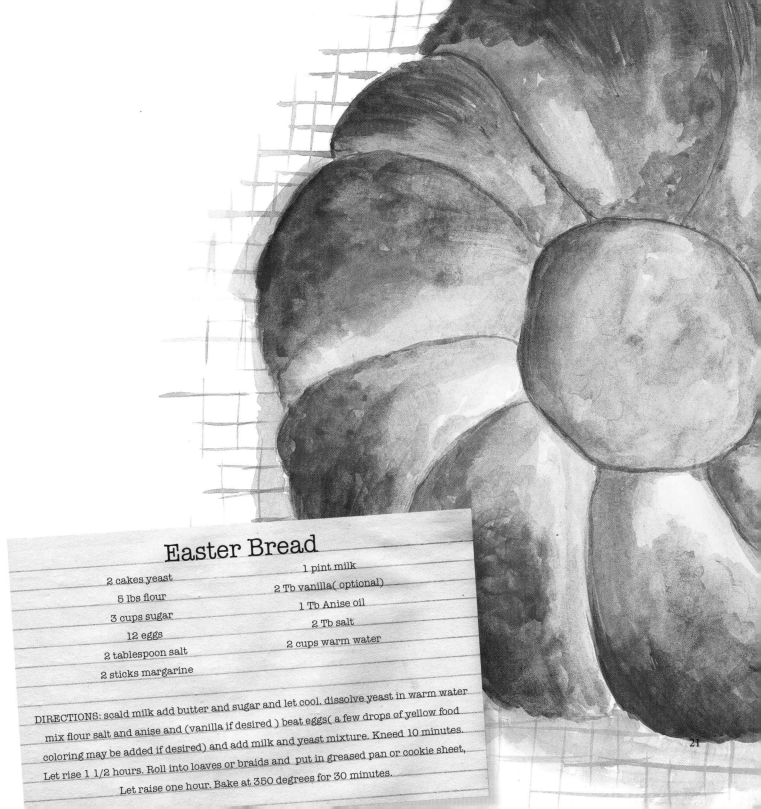

Easter Bread

2 cakes yeast

5 lbs flour

3 cups sugar

12 eggs

2 tablespoon salt

2 sticks margarine

1 pint milk

2 Tb vanilla(optional)

1 Tb Anise oil

2 Tb salt

2 cups warm water

DIRECTIONS: scald milk add butter and sugar and let cool. dissolve yeast in warm water mix flour salt and anise and (vanilla if desired) beat eggs(a few drops of yellow food coloring may be added if desired) and add milk and yeast mixture. Kneed 10 minutes. Let rise 1 1/2 hours. Roll into loaves or braids and put in greased pan or cookie sheet, Let raise one hour. Bake at 350 degrees for 30 minutes.

After church, Uncle John had Easter eggs ready for us to hunt. I could not wait for Easter dinner to be over so I could bite into that chocolate Easter Bunny!

In the summer, more cousins and aunts and uncles came to visit. They would stay at my grandparent's house and with us. We played outdoors until evening and then caught lightning bugs. There were no electronic games to play and the television we had only had a few black and white TV shows to watch. Sometimes the TV reception was bad and someone had to go outside to adjust the antennae to get a better picture on the screen.

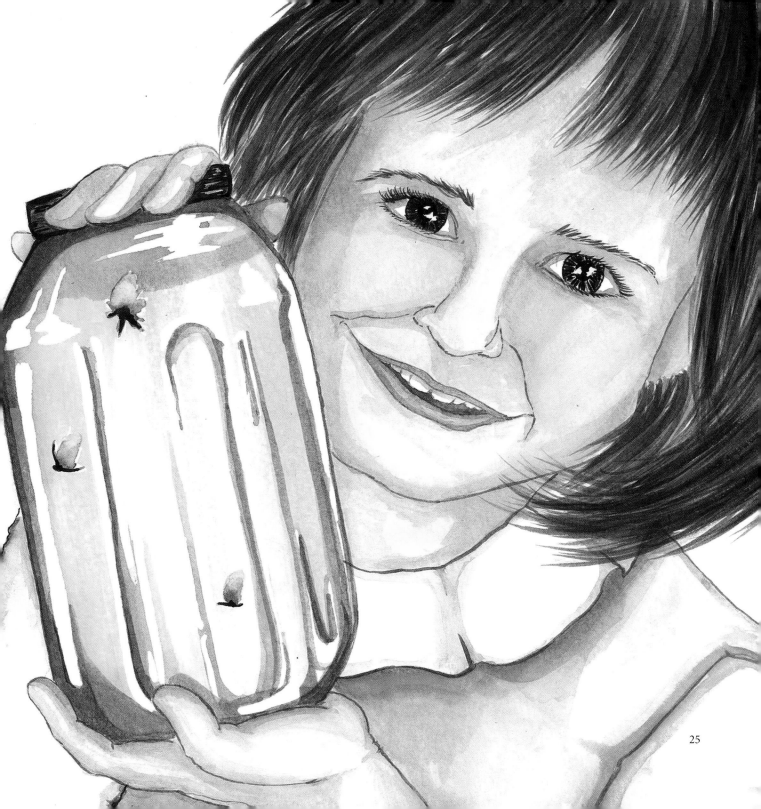

The only bad part about everyone coming to visit was they had to leave and go home. Everyone cried when they left because we knew it would be another whole year before we saw them again.

Birthdays were special. My family celebrated our birthdays with cake and ice cream of course, and we always had a whole meal, too. Not only could I invite my friends to my birthday party, but also all of my aunts, uncles, cousins and grandparents came, too. Sometimes they brought some of the food.

29

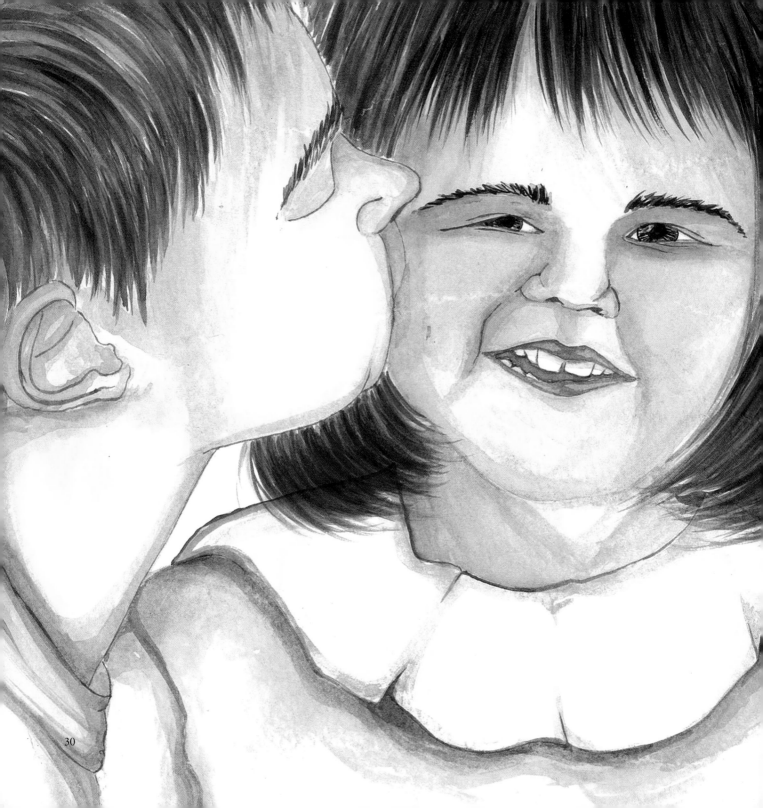

Any time my relatives came to my house or left, they got a hug and a kiss. The same thing happened when we left their house. Sometimes telling everyone good bye took longer than the visit!

What wonderful memories I have of growing up in my very special Italian family!

Aunt Sarah's Gallets

(Italian cookie) recipe:

Ingredients:
5 cups flour (sifted)
1 lb butter
3 1/2 cups brown sugar
1 T baking powder
8-10 eggs
1T vanilla

1. Cream butter, then add sugar and egg yolks, baking powder, vanilla and flour. Mix batter until very creamy.

2. Beat egg whites until stiff and add to the mixture.

3. Refrigerate overnight.

4. Drop by spoonful onto preheated waffle or gallett maker about a minute or until lightly browned.

Stuffed Shells

(as I was taught by my mother)

Ingredients:
your own favorite spaghetti sauce
one pound Jumbo Shells
1 cup ricotta cheese
1 1/2 cup grated Parmesan cheese
8 ounces shredded mozzarella
1 egg
2 teaspoons of parsley
season to taste with garlic salt and pepper

1. Cook the jumbo shells, rinse and drain.

2. In a separate bowl combine the ricotta cheese, Parmesan cheese, parsley and mozzarella cheese. Add the egg to the mixture and mix well. Season with garlic salt and pepper. Place one spoonful of filling in each shell.

3. In a 9x13 baking dish cover the pan with your favorite spaghetti sauce (using half), arrange the shells in the dish and cover with the remainder of your sauce. Sprinkle the top with Parmesan cheese and bake in a preheated 350 degree oven for 20 minutes.